# LEVEL UP!

## VISIONING YOUR LEADERSHIP DNA

Special <u>FREE</u> Bonus Gift for You!
To help you earn more revenue in your business,
I am offering a FREE Bonus.
Go to www.RoyceTalks.com
And request a resource guide on
Press Releases

ALL RIGHTS RESERVED. No part of this book or its associated ancillary materials may be reproduced or transmitted in any form or by any means, electronic or mechanical, including photocopying, recording, or any informational storage systems without permission from the publisher.

Disclaimer and/or legal notices. While all attempts have been made to verify information provided in this book and its ancillary materials, neither the author or publisher assumes any responsibility for errors, inaccuracies, or omissions and is not responsible for any financial loss by customer in any manner. This book is not intended for use as a source of legal or financial advice. If advice in these areas is needed, the services of a qualified professional should be sought.

Published by: RoyceTalks, LLC

Printed in the United States

Copyright © 2019 RoyceTalks

ISBN: 9781688129894

## Raving Fans……

"Royce is an amazing example of leading with authenticity. She has built her success through her strong interpersonal skills and leveraging her network. She knows how to be fully present and ask the right questions when networking to maximize relationships. I've had the privilege of networking with Royce for years and you can always count on her to be genuine and humble."--Allison (Ally) Jencson, Top Cat, Untame the Tigress

"Royce's engaging, inclusive spirit is matched by her actionable advice to help intergenerational co-founders prosper." Jim Sugarman, Co-Founder, 4GenNow

"Our collaborative work on the Women of Influence podcasts was rewarding, meaningful, and inspirational. Your vitality in the marketing space is refreshing and uplifting."--Lori Lovato, Amp Active Media

"Wow! I'm speechless! No words to describe your work. Thank you. I would love to work with you again. Your words inspire people; I'm not kidding."--Wayne B, cosmetic company founder

"I want to thank you for your amazing work. The blog received a lot of views today after I posted it. I referred you to my friend who publishes a magazine. He was so impressed with your writing."--Mauricio Henderson, Perseverance Staffing

"I highly recommend Royce as a marketing consultant. I have seen the impact of marketing strategies she has designed and implemented for companies and non-profit organizations that helped them overcome existing challenges, identify new opportunities, and position them to thrive in a dynamic market place. She's passionate about helping businesses identify their unique strengths, build their customer base, and establish brand loyalty. Royce will help you kick your business into high gear."--Sylvia Jennings, Owner Berkshire Hathaway Home Services

#Share

To order large quantities of this book for your

Employees or association, fill out the contact form at:
www.RoyceTalks.com

Royce Gomez may be the ideal speaker for your next event!
Any organization, association, or corpormation who wants to provide knowledge to help their team generate more revenue may want to consider inviting Royce for a keynote or workshop training.

To book Royce to speak:
www.RoyceTalks.com
719-684-4676

# TABLE OF CONTENTS

Secret #1...Dream Big!

Secret #2 .... Enroll Others

Secret #3....Believe in Yourself

Secret #4....Instant Gratification

Secret #5.....Online Dating and Leadership

Secret #6.....Failures Help Build the Pillars of Success

Secret #7.....Lessons From the Lake

Secret #8......Lake Lessons Continued

Secret #9......The Mt. Everest of Business

Secret #10....Living, Loving, Serving

Secret #11....Understand What's Important to YOU!!

Secret #12....Find Balance

Secret #13....Leadership Is Contagious

Secret #14....Ask!!

Secret #15....Be Positive

Secret #16....Think Creatively

Secret #17....Exude Confidence

Secret #18....Have Integrity

Secret #19....Inspire Others

Secret #20....Be Approachable

Secret #21....Be Committed

Secret #22....Delegate

Secret #23....Focus

Secret #24....Be Bold!

Secret #25....Have Passion

Secret #26....Resilience

Secret #27....Persistence

Bonus Chapters Originally published on SelfGrowth.com

Acknowledgments

## Visioning Your Leadership DNA

What makes one a leader?

Are you born a leader or do you develop the skills to be a leader?

Do you choose to be a leader or are you chosen?

I am writing to you as a child who was chosen last in gym class, overweight and wore hand-me-down clothes quite often. Although an introvert and an outcast as a child, those around me inadvertently called me into leadership. I remember from an early age my Sunday School teachers asking me to lead in small ways such as taking attendance or writing the memory verse on the board. My elementary school teachers would ask similar requests of me. These may seem small; but, a teacher has authority and who she chooses to do these tasks is looked at as a leader.

Being called to stand up at the front of the class and speak are the skills that are practiced for public speaking and used later in life when you become a leader in your career, civic group, or other area of your adult life. Strangely, although we practice these baby steps early on to become public speakers, we grow up to become adults who are uncomfortable with public speaking.

Fear and pride get in the way. Pride, you say? Yes! We all want to look good; our pride is hurt when we make a mistake or aren't accepted.

During my college years, I worked a full-time job and once again was called into leadership. At 19 I became assistant manager of a retail clothing store overseeing a staff of approximately 35, many of whom were twice my age. The age disparity made some jealous and I immediately had to learn more leadership skills to navigate the waters of jealousy and anger.

One lady in particular challenged me with her schedule, showing up on time, and helping with cleaning duties at closing time. She had a rebuttal for any directive I gave. All because there was jealousy due to my age being half hers, yet in authority over her.

Years later I moved my family to another state, starting over and knowing no one. Within a few months I was called to lead a group of over 100 homeschoolers, both students and their parents, to develop classes each semester. Again, I was called into leadership by my peers. Although the peers were more well-known and had been in the community much longer than I, I was called to lead and grew the organization rapidly.

Within a year we'd doubled in size and were receiving community recognition. I had done so well that eight years later when I stepped down, I begged someone to take over.

Tip: a good leader must groom other leaders to lead.

Stepping into a new life in another state the ultimate test of leadership came. I adopted a wild, untouched mustang, and had to prove to her that I was worthy of leading her and earning her trust.

I had moved from Chicago to Colorado, and had the opportunity to fulfill my lifelong dream of horse ownership. I'm sure the pros don't recommend diving in with little experience to train a wild mustang. But, during an impromptu moment I fell in love and adopted her.

Knowing nothing about training horses, I immersed myself in watching the experts, bought books, and gained knowledge any way possible. Through trial and error and building a relationship, I established myself as a leader of this wild mustang. The process was so rewarding and I went on to train more. But she and I had a lasting, special bond.

Today I have adult children who often recognize me as their mentor and role model, once again terms for "leader". Looking back this has been my title for many years, yet I have unusually not intentionally sought the role. So let's look at what qualities it takes to be a leader and some anecdotes to support each quality.

# Chapter 1
# Dream Big!!!

I know it sounds facetious. Everyone says dream big. Some will dispute that dreams mean nothing; it's action that makes the difference. Both are true, I believe. If you dispute this hang in here with me a minute.

You must dream. This is the fire that invigorates you to move to action. And, once you know what you dream about doing, you can work backwards from that BIG dream and set goals that will get you there. Once you set goals that will put you in the position to achieve your dream, you can delegate tasks that are necessary for you to achieve each goal. That's where the action comes in.

Have you ever seen anyone in action; but, not getting anywhere? You know the people on a five year plan ten years later…..? These are the people that are continually telling you how busy they are, yet never accomplishing anything. Why? Because they are busy working toward an unknown; they've never identified what their dream is. Therefore, they don't know what they are working for. Or perhaps you know someone on the "gold watch" plan. They work for a major corporation or a government entity and they go to work everyday, in action, complaining that they are unhappy. They are in action; but, long ago forgot how to dream.

This is why I believe it does indeed take both a dream and action. But, without a BIG dream the actions are useless.

One of my guests on *Thrive: A Woman's Journey to Victory* said that she walked into her first interview for her current role and was asked where she wanted to be in five years. Her response was that she wanted to be in charge. Although she didn't know what that entailed or if she was qualified for the role of leader, having the necessary skill sets to carry out the required tasks, she knew her dream was big enough she could learn. And, she did!

I was working on an important project at one time. I had a BIG dream seeing myself as an international speaker and coach. One action step I knew I had to take when I broke down the goals necessary to achieve my dream was to schedule twelve speakers in three months for my radio show. The goal determined that I needed to have one guest per week to increase the number of my regular listeners. Within three weeks of setting that goal I had scheduled thirteen speakers by simply asking (more about that in a later chapter!).

The power of a BIG dream ignites the fire in you to set goals and develop an action plan. Being a leader is who you are, not how you feel or what your title is. You can be a leader whether you are the janitor or CEO. Feelings come and go; but, they don't define who you are. A leader is a leader and has a BIG dream that lets everyone know where he's headed and enrolls others around him who help him achieve it.

Some people believe in vision boards or dream boards. I did my first dream board in the late 80's at the suggestion of a mentor. It was filled with expensive, material possessions, and although not wrong, remember to include your why. Today I still have expensive things I want, such as a 100-day trip to Europe. However, today my "why" is to spend quality time with people I love and appreciate the beauty of other cultures. Whereas before it was simply to impress.

There is no right or wrong, and ultimately you decide why your dreams are important, however I challenge you to get a "why" that motivates you.

# Chapter 2
# Enroll Others

In chapter one I alluded to the fact that a BIG dream has so much power that it will enroll others in your life. They can't help it; they become touched, moved and inspired. Every successful person I've met or interviewed has resolutely said they would not be where they are today if it weren't for the help of others.

When you share your dream, vision, or whatever you are comfortable calling it, you share it with such passion and life within your words you inspire anyone within earshot. They become enrolled and doors are opened to you that you never even imagined.

Let me share a glimpse of that from my book, *The Spontaneous Journey*. In 2015 my BIG dream was to travel. Simply travel as much as possible with no particular plan in place. However, I knew Nashville was one place on my bucket list because of the food, music and startup ecosystem that was brewing strongly there. I set and achieved the goal of making it to Nashville, and while there attended quite a few networking events. During one particular event, I met a woman who worked at a social enterprise. Social enterprise businesses are of particular interest to me so I asked if I could tour the company's headquarters (once again I ASKED; this will be talked about in a later chapter!). Without hesitation she said "yes" and we scheduled a time for me to take a tour.

At the end of the tour we were sitting at her desk and I saw a chart listing upcoming trips they were taking stakeholders and volunteers on. One of the destinations was Costa Rica, another place on my bucket list. I shared this along with my expertise of writing stories telling of the community impact organizations were making, and consulting social enterprise business models. The next thing you know she was so enrolled in my BIG dream of travelling, she invited me to Costa Rica to cover the story of this particular trip. My BIG dream had the power to enroll others whether for a season or a lifetime. In this particular instance, our paths crossed for a brief season; but, the impact lasted for a lifetime.

Enrolling others is crucial to success as a leader. You will never achieve greatness without enrolling others. True leaders know they don't make it by themselves; it takes enrolling others. This can mean hiring them, asking for their mentorship, meeting with them occasionally for support and encouragement, asking outright for specific help or a plethora of other ways. Whichever way you engage others, you'll only become a leader when you enroll others in your journey.

# Chapter 3
# Believe in Yourself

Without believing in yourself, you won't achieve what you are capable of. Oftentimes we see those who have come from circumstances that leave them at a disadvantage to achieve great success, and others will believe in them before they will believe in themselves. Sometimes we'll see someone from a privileged background that never had to struggle to get what they wanted, and when they suddenly set a goal to strike out on their own, they don't have the fortitude. Their belief quickly wanes.

Whatever your background, circumstances, perceived advantages or disadvantages, I can guarantee you don't believe in yourself to the extent that you could. You think smaller than you should; you are playing a smaller game than you are capable of. I've spoken to people who make $30,000 a year and those who believe they are wildly successful because they are multi-millionaires. Before you get offended about me saying "who believe", I applaud you for achieving the 1% club and you ARE wildly successful. But, I am willing to bet if you look back at your journey before you joined the 1% club, you were stretched. At one time you had a conversation with a mentor who said, *"Are you sure you are thinking big enough? I bet you can do more!"* Because they made that statement, you either had an immediate thought of *"No, I can't!"* or *"Hmmmm……..."* and you looked at it and expanded your original vision.

*I've often heard some version of the paraphrase:*
*"You will never achieve more than what you believe you can achieve"*

I would tend to agree with Oprah Winfrey who said *"You become what you believe."*

And that *"Limitations live only within our minds. But if we use our imaginations, our possibilities become limitless."* --Jamie Paolinetti

And the successful legend, Henry Ford, who stated, *"Whether you think you can or think you can't, you're right!"*

No matter what level of success you are at or what circumstances you face, I invite you to look at what you believe about yourself.

One of the articles I published revealed a time when I looked back at the time in my life when I was working from home while raising my kids. Although I was an entrepreneur and running a mildly successful business, I saw myself as a "mom" and "housewife", not as an accomplished businesswoman. All three roles were true; but, it was the belief of only being a mom and housewife that hindered my ability to succeed and achieve the goals I had for myself and my business. In conclusion, I don't think it's enough to believe in yourself; but, also believe in an accurate identity of ourselves because as Oprah said we become what we believe.

# Chapter 4
# Instant Gratification

Leaders understand there is no such thing as instant gratification. Although Forbes Magazine shared these statistics recently:

If an online video takes longer than 10 seconds to load, 85% of online users will leave Google searches for same day shipping is up 120% since 2015 and consumers are willing to pay considerably more to have it delivered same day
Google also reports that searches for same day flights and hotels are up 150% in the last 2 years
Being in such a society makes it difficult to wait on results, and persevere to achieve said results.

I believe leaders understand the natural cycle of seeing things come to fruition.

First, I believe a dream within us is stirred. We see a vision of what we want to achieve.

I remember in 2001 having a vision of using horses to minister to the hurting and broken. But, even before that time, I believe a seed was planted. Let's back up in the story and see if you can see it.

As a young girl I longed for a horse. Knowing I couldn't have one, I lived vicariously through stories. Mom would take me to the library and I would find every novel available that had a horse on the cover or mention of a young child owning a horse. I devoured every story I could, imagining it was me in that story; I would even cry if the animal died during the story.

Then as a young, married woman other women who were hurting found their way to me, seeking advice and comfort. I spent hours consoling, guiding, leading them to wholeness. This continued for decades.

Finally, both of these longings came together in 2001. I began using horses to give riding lessons to young children. Out of this was birthed other programs, including programs working with at-risk youth and women who had suffered domestic violence and other trauma.

Although the dream was stirred in me as a child, there are two other seasons to note here.

The second season is a season of waiting. I longed for a horse as far back as I can remember; I was in my mid-30s when I finally bought my first horse.

The waiting season was long, but necessary. Everything that happened in between helped shape what that dream looked like. The waiting prepared me. It tested me to determine if this dream really mattered to me. Oftentimes, waiting can show us that something we're waiting for isn't important.

Have you ever watched a child in September? The commercials come out for all the latest Christmas toys. Your child begins to watch with anticipation. He sees the newest toys come out; and the commercials highlight all the reasons your child must have this toy. They begin to beg and plead with you for the toy. As Christmas draws near they tell Santa they want the toy they've coveted for the last three months. Christmas morning comes, and they unwrap that all-consuming toy. Yet, a week later and that toy is set aside, forgotten.

You see, it's in the waiting that you are shaped, developed and tested to determine if this dream is worthy of your attention and devotion.

When it finally comes to fruition, there is a sense of awe, surprise, and wonder at how suddenly the season of waiting has ended and the dream is now a reality.

As I examine the seasons of my life and speak to dozens of successful people, they all say that success didn't happen overnight. Although they may not say it in these words, they clearly see where a dream was planted, a season of waiting, and finally the realization of that dream coming to pass.

Why is it then that so often we get frustrated, angry and anxious when our dream doesn't become reality instantaneously. We begin to doubt, create a "Plan B", or other solutions we feel we need. This only detours us from the path we were created for.

So many women I coach as they approach mid-life lament to me that they feel their years were wasted in their career. They are searching for their meaning, purpose, "true north",........It's called so many things. Ultimately, we want to chase our dream, and when it seemingly eludes us, we doubt.

# Chapter 5
# Online Dating and Leadership

Online dating. What does that have to do with leadership? To answer that question, let's look at the ultimate goal of online dating. I'll assume for a moment that you are drawn to online dating in the hopes to find your soul mate, your forever someone.

If you aren't looking for marriage, you are looking for a short-term relationship to fulfil social needs. Either way, you are looking for some kind of connection.

Leaders look for connection too. A leader understands that only through connecting can he engage his employees, build a long-term relationship to promote from within, and mentor those who have potential to contribute more.

A leader doesn't underestimate the power of connection. And, oftentimes a leader understands there are seasons for him to groom a mentee then send the mentee on his way to accomplish bigger and better things. Through his connection he has watered a plant that blooms far beyond what it thought it could.

People long to be connected with, understood, mentored or watered, so to speak.

Online dating shows us that longing for connection will sometimes draw us to take a pseudo-relationship over loneliness. We'll hang on to that pseudo-relationship until a real connection, one that positions us for long-term growth, security, and connectedness, comes along.

As a leader you can make someone feel used, as one does after being in a shallow, pseudo-relationship or you can make someone feel valuable and connected, as one does when he finally finds "the one", the real connection and long-term commitment.

Be the leader who truly connects with others and helps a mentee blossom with untapped, un-seen potential. They will remember you; you will have a lasting impact.

# Chapter 6
# Failures Help Build the Pillars of Success

As an entrepreneur, you aspire to be successful. You have ideas that you want to expand on and build into something great. Whether success means fame and fortune or maybe it means success on a smaller scale, it is important to you, yet defined differently by all.

Richard Branson is one of those successful entrepreneurs having become a well-known billionaire who lives on his own island retreat. He created the "Virgin" brand. Whether it's Virgin Atlantic, Virgin Money, Virgin Media, Virgin Trains or another of his endless Virgin lines, his brand is seen and recognized by everyone. His success can be used as an inspiration to you, an aspiring entrepreneur, as you work hard to create your own success.

Branson is quoted as saying, "Do not be embarrassed by your failures, learn from them and start again." This means that in his experience, success did not always come easy. It was something he had to work for.

In fact, success usually comes with a price. That includes failures, which in the long run, lead you to where you want to be. Even Branson had a number of **failures** when it came to the Virgin business. As he says in his quote though, he didn't let it stop him from trying new ideas. He wasn't embarrassed to try and try again.

Branson failed at creating a drink line, a wedding dress line, fashion line, cosmetics line, a music player, social media website and more. Still, despite all those failures, he remains to be one of the most wildly successful entrepreneurs in the world. His brand remains to be one of the most recognized. When you fail, you might get discouraged in your work or your purpose and your attitude may falter. That may lead you to give up. You may dwell on everything that went wrong and wonder why you should continue.

You can't let failure get in the way of the multitude of successes you will achieve by pursuing your dream. You may feel like you have hit rock bottom. You just have to get yourself back up and stand on your feet.

Instead of looking at your failure as the absolute bottom, try to view your failure as an elevator. Your goal is to make it to the top floor to reach success, but you've made a mistake and you hit the wrong button so you've ridden the elevator back down a floor or two. Now is your chance to learn from your mistake, your failure, and choose the right button instead the second time around.

You won't make the same mistake of pressing the wrong button because you've already done that once before and you've seen the consequences. If you take the time to consider your failures and learn from your mistakes, you can start to ride the elevator back to the top again -- to your success. That's not to say there won't be many mistakes throughout your lifetime. We are only human, after all. But how else are we going to learn? Take every mistake and look at it as a blessing. Without it, you would never know you did something wrong. Then you can take that mistake and transform it into something positive and advance forward. Take **these other famous** entrepreneurs, for example. They have known failure and yet they continued to try. Arianna Huffington was rejected by publishers 37 times and still has the Huffington Post. Bill Gates failed with his first company and yet managed to create Microsoft. Walt Disney was told he lacked creativity and now his work is known by everyone. Milton Hershey had to go through three candy companies before Hershey's chocolate was a success. The list goes on and on. But today, these entrepreneurs have overcome their failures and made a name for themselves. They continued to try even after they were told that they couldn't or they faced a failure.

They persisted, and that's really what matters most. If you strive to be the best entrepreneur that you can be, then you can't help but succeed.

Most entrepreneurs could tell you that their successes are rooted in failure. Though they didn't let that stop them from pursuing their dreams and becoming successful because of it. Use their work as an example to yourself. Though failure may be disappointing and a hard lesson to learn, there is still success to be had. Failure is part of success.

# Chapter 7
# Lessons From the Lake

As I moved down the street from a lake, the first goal I set was learning to kayak. Being that I'm not athletic and not that fond of being in water--especially cold water with stuff swimming in it--I didn't want to invest in a new kayak. I figure the loss would be more palatable if I bought it used, went out once, and didn't like it, I could easily sell it and get my investment back.

And, since I had never been in a kayak before in my life, did I want the sit-in or sit-on kayak? Which was easier to learn with? Which was safer?

I searched the ads regularly until one day the opportunity presented itself to get a good deal, and the guy had both the sit-in and sit-on versions. Unfortunately, it was hard to choose sitting in them in his driveway, dry docked. But, after a bit of interrogation, I made the choice and took home my gently used kayak at a good price.

I went home and watched less than 15 minutes of YouTube videos on the basics of kayaking. I felt I understood how to enter the boat and use the oars well enough to keep myself from tipping over on the first try. The first time I went out in the new kayak, I only tried it out for about 10 minutes. I had no life jacket and no license on the boat and didn't want to risk harm to me or consequences for breaking the law; I simply wanted to see if I thought I was going to like my new sport.

The second time I went out a bit longer, just trying to get more proficient at rowing and controlling my direction. In that moment I looked across the lake and said "By the end of summer, about 8 weeks away, I am going to be able to row across the lake." Not being athletic and being self-taught with YouTube videos I figured that was a reasonable goal.

Well, the sixth time I went out, I had logged less than 3 hours of kayaking time. The wind was slightly gusty, causing the water to be a bit choppy. I was out there mid-day after working diligently all morning and feeling a sense of accomplishment. Taking a look across the lake, I said resolutely "Today is the day I'll cross the lake."

I began to cross the lake from south to north and the winds made the current work against me. Quickly I decided to go from southwest to east. I paddled quickly, almost feeling the kayak glide across the water. A grin spread across my face, my chest puffed out, and I began to row faster and faster. I could see the finish line and was proud of myself and the ability to learn my new sport so quickly!

I got across the lake and my arms ached since I actively rowed against the wind. For a few minutes I sat quietly and allowed myself to relish in my victory. Then I decided it was time to head back.

Just then a stronger wind picked up and I was rowing against the wind. It was almost as if I had to row twice as hard to move the kayak forward while the wind pushed it back. But, kayaking is an individual sport and I had to make it back on my own efforts. So I rowed hard and fast. As I rowed hard and fast I realized that it was probably the first time I had rowed as the video instructed me to. I stuck the oars deep into the water, did a full semi-circle row, and gave it my all.

It was in this moment I realized that learning to kayak had shown me some lessons which were relevant to building a business.

The take-aways may seem minor to an experienced entrepreneur who has led teams to victory before, but to the one who is learning business as a new sport, and becoming a leader, here they are:

First, instruction or coaching is vital to not making mistakes that will turn you over in the deep water.

Second, have a business plan. Just like I investigated and inquired sit-in or sit-on and searched for a good deal, you need to have a plan of what you want to accomplish and the price you are willing to pay for it.

Third, I set a goal to get across the lake. Some may set the same goal for their first attempt at kayaking, others may work a year to achieve it. It doesn't matter. You are in competition with no one. It's your goal; no one else's. Set a goal you feel good about and work towards it. If, like me, you are an overachiever and you accomplish it early, set a new goal. Or perhaps look to see if you set the bar too low because you had doubts, fears, or limiting beliefs. Maybe I could have made it across the lake the first time I kayaked after I registered the boat and felt legal. But, I didn't believe I could.
Fourth, I enjoyed several trips out onto the lake, and meandered about casually. It wasn't until I was out there alone with the wind tossing me about that I got serious about my technique and rowed with all the power and competence I could muster. And, it was then that I learned the biggest lesson to share with you through my adventures on the lake…..

Finally, although you have a coach who has given you instructions, it's up to you to implement what you were taught. And, it's up to you to do it well and finish well. You see, I was out there on the lake and had to return to the dock no matter what. No one was coming to rescue me or do it for me. Although the wind wasn't strong enough I needed rescued, I'm making a point here. When the waters of business get rough, it's up to you to sink or swim. It's up to you to arrive safely back to shore.

I'd be remiss if I didn't share with you that I thoroughly enjoy kayaking and am looking to invest in a second one---one short week after buying my first. Why? To take others out so we can spend time building relationships and allowing them to learn lessons from the lake. It may be that they have fears, doubts, and limiting beliefs they can overcome on the lake. Or perhaps, they need to unwind and learn to enjoy the view on the journey. I don't know what you need to learn to become the leader you are called to be, but perhaps taking up a new sport will reveal lessons meant solely for you. Ahoy, matey!

# Chapter 8
# Lake Lessons Continued

## Lessons From the Kayak Continued

As you move forward in your ability, it requires learning new skills and continuing to educate yourself. Whether we are talking about kayaking or business, this is true.
After I crossed the lake, I realized there were other skills I needed to learn. Large fish were jumping around my kayak. What if one hit my boat and tipped me into the water? What if one jumped, and landed right in my lap? My 15 minutes of watching YouTube videos only gave me the basics, not training to overcome challenges on the water.

Business is similar in that often you can start your business, build it to an acceptable level, but now other challenges come and you don't have solutions for them. As a leader in your organization it is critical you never stop educating yourself and getting an instructor or coach to help you reach the next level.

Challenges come and you navigate rougher waters; it takes a leader to humble himself and ask for instructions or an outside perspective.

I won't tell you how to handle a fish jumping in your lap while kayaking because my novice advice isn't worth two cents. However, as a leader with over two decades of experience leading teams, making mistakes, being the lone wolf, and handling situations with below average tact and knowledge, I can say life works better when you have others providing you feedback to navigate the rough waters of leadership.

# Chapter 9
# The Mt. Everest of Business

I went to a conference for startup founders, and before the conference began, at the table of coffee and muffins a man caught my eye. He had energy when he came near you, and he had a story to tell. We sat and talked for quite some time and his story was so intriguing I told him I was writing a book and had to share his story.

My new friend from the conference, Brooke Chesnut, has graciously allowed me to share his story with you, and he travels to share his story with corporations because what he learned was transferable to leadership lessons, specific to HR Directors and C-suite executives.

Brooke is an avid climber and spends his time seeking out the next 14er he wants to conquer. Because he's connected to a lot of climbers, he booked a trip to climb Mt. Everest. Brooke trained harder and longer than most and felt like he was in the best shape of his life when he departed for his trip to climb Mt. Everest.

To climb Mt. Everest, there is base camp, Camps #1-4, and finally the summit. He arrived and his daughter accompanied him for the three weeks they are required to stay at base camp to acclimate and get connected to your Sherpa.

Brooke spent these three weeks mentoring other climbers on layering their clothing to create thermal warmth. His daughter spent time posting pictures to social media. From this he was booked to be a keynote. The person who hired him knew what he was doing, and to some extent how, but he didn't know why. Your people want to know why they need to strive for excellence in their job. As a leader, share your why with them; it motivates and engages them.

Lesson number one from the climb is acclimate. Familiarize yourself with the climate. The climbers spent 14 days from the airport to base camp. Things were done systematically for the safety of the climbers. After all, for the next eight weeks their home and bed would be on the rock, snow, and ice.

Oftentimes a new leader is hired and he wants to take the company from base camp to camp 3; on the mountain you die if you attempt this. In business, your culture and organizational structure can die if you try to make changes without acclimatizing your people gradually. Forcing "camp 3" can set your team up for failure.

The climbers go up and down for a month. Think of these climbers as people on your corporate team: they all have great resumes, they've paid the same price to get where they are, and they've trained for this moment. Yet, even after paying the price, four climbers left before they ascended out of base camp. They were under-prepared and knew it.

When you think of the recruiting process, you are like a Sherpa, asking after they are on the job, "Are you OK?" Acclimatization is the foundation for success.

The second lesson Brooke shared with me from his climb is how important community is. Base camp isn't even on the mountain yet. The Sherpa goes through a ritual of bringing in a llama and asking the mountain to grant its permission to do the climb. This ritual lasts four hours and is considered the most important day of the entire expedition.

It is the Sherpa's job to get the climber from camp 4 to the summit, yet they are brought in and introduced to the climbers during the ceremony to begin to build a sense of community. Camp 4 is still seven weeks away. For seven weeks the Sherpa delivers strength and humility daily. Who is the Sherpa in your company that delivers strength and humility to empower your people to keep climbing? What do you do to build community? The Sherpa walks alongside the climber for seven weeks.

Third, it is important to listen. Are you really listening to your people? The climbers shared how to pack bags for efficiency, clamp on boots to keep water out, shared what tea to drink when for optimal physical performance and health; it didn't matter who was more experienced. They all listened and shared with one another for the greater good of the team.

Brooke hit his stride on the way to camp 3. He was one of the oldest climbers and felt excluded. But, when he arrived in third place to camp 3 at 25,000 feet in altitude, he went from being excluded to being embraced and celebrated.

However, after all the training, mentoring other climbers, and arriving safely at 25,000 feet, Brooke took off his glove momentarily to adjust a boot and his fingers froze. At risk of losing his fingers, he was ordered off the mountain and transported to the local hospital. Brooke became indignant and unhappy that he had invested time and money to climb Mt. Everest and was told by his Sherpa he couldn't continue. He would not summit with the other climbers.

Today, however, Brooke takes these lessons to corporations and share his powerful, intriguing story and translates it to building better leaders. I am happy to call him friend from a fortuitous meeting one day.

# Chapter 10
# Living, serving, loving.

Here are some quotes from famous people, but first, let me share one of mine:

*"Thrive. You weren't designed to merely survive, but to thrive. Life life to the fullest. Carpe diem. Bring exuberant joy into the room. Love passionately. Serve thoughtfully. Thrive. Therein lies the secret to happiness and a life lived fully."--Royce Gomez*

*"Life is full of beauty. Notice it. Notice the bumble bee, the small child, and the smiling faces. Smell the rain, and feel the wind. Live your life to the fullest potential, and fight for your dreams."– Ashley Smith*

*"You are never too old to set another goal or to dream a new dream."– C.S. Lewis*

*"What is not started today is never finished tomorrow."– Johann Wolfgang von Goethe*

*"Dream as if you'll live forever, live as if you'll die today."– James Dean*

*"Like success, failure is many things to many people. With positive mental attitude, failure is a learning experience, a rung on the ladder, and a plateau at which to get your thoughts in order to prepare to try again."– W. Clement Stone*

*"No matter where you're from, your dreams are valid."– Lupita Nyong'o*

*"There are some people who live in a dream world, and there are some who face reality; and then there are those who turn one into the other."– Douglas H. Everett*

*"The only thing that will stop you from fulfilling your dreams is you."– Tom Bradley*

*"The only thing worse than starting something and failing ... is not starting something."* – Seth Godin

*"Dream no small dreams for they have no power to move the hearts of men."* – Johann Wolfgang von Goethe

*"When I'm old and dying, I plan to look back on my life and say, 'Wow, that was an adventure,' not, 'Wow, I sure felt safe.'"* – Tom Preston-Werner

*Don't wait. Make memories today. Celebrate your life! ~ unknown*
*Life has no limitations, except the ones you make. ~ Les Brown*

*Life is a great big canvas, and you should throw all the paint on it you can. ~ Danny Kaye*

*Don't be afraid your life will end; be afraid that it will never begin. ~ Grace Hansen*

*You only live once, but if you do it right, once is enough. ~ Joe Lewis*

*Somebody should tell us, right at the start of our lives, that we are dying. Then we might live life to the limit, every minute of every day. Do it! I say. Whatever you want to do, do it now! There are only so many tomorrows. ~* **Pope Paul VI**

*I don't wait for the calendar to figure out when I should live life. ~* **Gene Simmons**

*It is not the years in your life but the life in your years that counts. ~ Adlai Stevenson*

*"To accomplish great things, we must not only act, but also dream; not only plan, but also believe."* – Anatole France

*"There is only one thing that makes a dream impossible to achieve: the fear of failure."– Paulo Coelho*
*"It is only when we truly know and understand that we have a limited time on earth – and that we have no way of knowing when our time is up – that we will begin to live each day to the fullest, as if it was the only one we had."– Elizabeth Kubler-Ross*

*"It may be that those who do most, dream most."– Stephen Butler Leacock*

*"If one advances confidently in the direction of one's dreams, and endeavors to live the life which one has imagined, one will meet with a success unexpected in common hours."– Henry David Thoreau*

*"Whatever you do, or dream you can, begin it. Boldness has genius and power and magic in it."– Johann Wolfgang von Goethe*

# Chapter 11
# Understand What's Important to YOU!

It does no good to become successful if you don't remember what's truly important to you. And, as a leader it's your duty to know what is important to you. This becomes your guiding compass and allows those who follow you to align themselves with that.

There's a television show called *Undercover Boss* on CBS that would show executives going into the day-to-day lives of their employees and performing the mundane tasks of sales, maintenance, and other entry level jobs with their staff. Often the executives would admit they went in to fix some policies and procedures that would make their company more efficient and effective at carrying out a particular task, one that had caused either internal or external strife (code: a customer service nightmare!) in their organization. Instead what they learn is finding out what's important to them in the way they lead and the empathy gained for their employees. Whether it be implementing a procedure that makes a job more streamlined and provides a higher degree of teamwork, making for a happier employee, or whether it be to find their employee is so committed their work-life balance is compromised and they change their PTO (paid time off) policies, the employees always seem to benefit from the lessons learned as the CEO takes this journey.

Despite the outcome, one common thread is revealed as these undercover bosses return to their executive suite: they grasp what's important to them and revise the leadership they were giving before they spent a week in the field.

They say money doesn't change people; it reveals who they truly are. Sometimes as we climb the ladder of success we lose what's truly important to us.

While on vacation in St. Thomas, I met a bartender who left a Fortune 100 tech company with a six-figure salary, great benefits package, and a wonderful work culture she raved about as being one of the best in the country.

With all of these positive attributes of the job, why would she leave?

She left because she realized while on vacation there what was important to her was to live a relaxed lifestyle and grab her surfboard on a daily basis. This bartender went from a posh condo in a major metropolis with a six-figure income to sharing a small apartment and making enough to "get by" because of what's important to her. She was unable to live out what was truly important to her even though she had a great job and much satisfaction.

What's truly important to you? Once you define it are you creating a life that allows you to live it out?

Remember your why, live by your values, then the how will come.

# Chapter 12
# Find Balance

Find balance. What does that mean? It seems so trite, yet everyone has a different picture of what that means when they hear it. For some, they envision themselves in a meditative position. For others, they envision themselves taking weekends off. For others, it is finding time for friends. And yet others, for pursuing personal hobbies.

For the bartender who discovered what was truly important to her, balance meant living and playing on the beach daily. For the stay-at-home mom, it might be to make time for pampering and self-care one afternoon a week. Oops, did I lose you? Talking about stay-at-home moms in a leadership book is controversial to some. But, before you get wrapped up in your title, remember that anyone can be a leader. And, we can be put in a leadership role in our community, our church, our job, or our home. At some point in life, most of us are called to lead someone!

*"Balance comes in the moments when you stand up for the life you truly want for yourself, by making choices that align with that."--Unknown*

*"Balance is not better time management, but better boundary management. Balance means making choices and enjoying those choices."--Unknown*

*"Balance is not something you find. It's something you create."--Unknown*

What do these three quotes have in common? First, they point out the fact that you are personally responsible for balance. How? Through your choices. Second, balance requires that you know what you want. Only by knowing what you want can you create balance.

Finding balance is like finding rest. It doesn't happen on it's own. You must create it by making choices that allow it.

With certainty we know that balance is a choice you are personally responsible for creating. But, what exactly does balance look like?

*"It's all about quality of life and finding a happy balance between work and friends and family."--Philip Green*

I'd agree with Philip that balance looks a bit different for us all and what balance looks like today may not be how you define balance in a new season of your life. Perhaps you'll put more emphasis on family time with the birth of a new baby, children looking at colleges, or a spouse battling major illnesses. Work may get more of a priority when it's time to strive for a promotion or accept a partnership in the law firm.

Balance need not be a stagnant concept; but, one that evolves with life. Creating balance is about quality of life.

# Chapter 13
# Leadership is Contagious

Research has shown that being around someone who is happy gives you a 25% greater probability that you will be happier. The same with sadness. Emotions are contagious. You know this when you walk into a room and "feel" the mood. Behaviors are also contagious. If you are overweight, you are more likely to have close friends who are overweight. If you are divorced, you are much more likely to have divorced friends. When mom told you "You are who you hang around."there is much truth in that. You are very likely to surround yourself with those who have similar behaviors.

What does any of this have to do with a secret to becoming a great leader?

A study was done finding correlations of a 360 degree assessment between senior level management and mid-level management teams under the senior managers. The findings were astounding, showing significant correlation in 30 of 51 behaviors. Developing self and others, integrity, cooperation, strategic acumen and being focused on results are some of these behaviors that were contagious.

If you look at this list of contagious behaviors you'll see that your leadership can indeed create a team of lifelong learners who seek personal development. Your leadership can create a team that performs its tasks with integrity and cooperation, a.k.a. teamwork. Finally, if your team thought strategically and focused on results, your team would perform at a higher level delivering even greater results.

It's been said that A players hire A players while B players hire C players, presumably because they are insecure and want to be the "smartest person in the room". Therefore, they surround themselves with people who perform at a lower level than they do so they outshine them. However, the adverse effect is that you develop a lower functioning team. Whereas, if you hire A players, they will make you look good by outperforming your expectations.

A leader not only shares contagious behaviors and emotions, constantly causing his team to perform to exhibit the behaviors and emotions of one who succeeds, he also is secure enough in who he is. He surrounds himself with the best. He isn't threatened by others who are more experienced, smarter, more highly educated, or more accomplished than he, thus hiring C players. A great leader wants surrounded by the best with everyone contributing at their highest level.

You are contagious! Are you spreading the qualities of a great leader?

*"The measure of a leader is the behavior of his followers"*--Aubrey Daniels

# Chapter 14
# Ask!

I've alluded to this in other chapters, now let's dive in! A leader is courageous enough to ASK!
Yes!

How many people do you know who go out to eat and won't ask the server for a drink refill or to have their steak cooked the way they want it? This seems small and insignificant and maybe you are wondering what that has to do with leadership, but it does. If you won't ask for a refill on water, how will you ever ask for a raise?

Let's look at the power of asking through some personal stories.

When I started my radio show I knew I wanted to ask some friends I admired, but the world didn't know about, and I wanted to ask my co-authors, another accomplished but obscure group of people, to appear as guests. But, what about asking someone like an international speaker or an up-and-coming musician that will eventually be known? I looked at my connections on my social media platforms and found prospects like that and asked them. Guess what? They said "yes!".

Attending the Tin Pan festival one year, we barely got in. My mom and I were one of the last five people in the venue with a standing room only crowd. I knew my mom was unable to stand through the entire show so when a man walked up to me and asked if he could help, I said "yes". We were seated next to the TV network that was covering the event. Here we were just normal people sitting among the media and industry leaders. And those connections led to future business for me.

This leads me to another tip on mindset. You always belong. To believe you are any less because you are "normal" while they are the "leaders" or "experts", and you have a mindset issue. You belong if you are willing to put yourself at their table.

A mentor once told me a parable of eating at the kids table versus the adult table. In a large family, the kids sit at their own table. One day you become of age where you don't want to sit at the kids table any longer; you want to graduate to the adult table. But, if there are no seats left, you are stuck at the kids table. In life, sometimes we never graduate to the adult table with adult conversations because we feel we don't belong. This isn't a problem of belonging; it's a problem of mindset, of believing you don't belong.

Another time I was offered a contract to do some consulting with startups. The organization was young and the pay was lower than I should accept given my experience. However, I asked them to provide housing as part of the package. They conceded, and that enabled me to stay in a beach house with amazing sunset views on the water during the time I was hired to consult. I was rewarded with a beautiful setting and a huge cost savings not having to rent a furnished apartment just by asking.

The Bible tells us God wants to give us more than we can ask or imagine. What can you imagine asking for? I challenge you to ask for more than that!

Leaders who are confident and courageous enough to ask for what they want often get it.

In sales they often teach you to propose three asks: a small, medium and large sale. The philosophy is that your customer will choose one of the three and you'll never get a "no". Imagine getting more yeses. That is every salesperson's dream!

Whether a salesperson or leader, the power of asking will result in more than you currently have. You may be shocked to find most people willing to comply. Be a courageous leader and ASK!

# Chapter 15
Be Positive

In a previous chapter I mentioned emotions are contagious. When you walk into a room where others have had a strong disagreement you feel it. When you join a celebration, you know it. Both of those rooms have distinctly different vibes. Therefore, if emotions are contagious, as a leader, it's vital for you to be positive.

When you are leading others and displaying a positive attitude it truly is contagious. Some of the results include:

Less complaining
Increased productivity
Greater engagement
Increased loyalty to both you and the organization
Open communication
More creativity

Aren't these results you want with your team? Corporations pay thousands of dollars for corporate trainers to come in and improve morale, productivity and engagement. Yet, you can accomplish a significant change in these areas simply by having a positive attitude.

Let's look at Seth, a manager who supervises a team of eight. Seth comes in on Monday morning complaining about all that went wrong over the weekend. He walks over to his desk and sees the unfinished pile of reports that are due by lunch today. This starts him on a new rant that there is too much to do and expectations are too high. How do those eight feel that are listening? Chances are the room has become quiet. Everyone has their head down pretending they are working. When Seth gets up to fill his coffee cup, the murmur quickly elevates with the eight gossiping until Seth walks their way. Again, the room quiets. Not productive, right?

Now imagine Seth walking in on Monday morning with a cheerful smile on his face and greeting all as he passes. As he greets each employee he delegates a task to them that will help him complete his reports. He asks them to deliver their assignment to him within 30 minutes. Before the hour is up everyone has turned in their assignment, he thanks them and turns the completed reports into his boss before noon. Each team member goes to lunch chatting about great teamwork.

A different attitude. A different conversation. And a different result.

What was the catalyst for this? It all started with a positive attitude. Leaders are human and they experience the range of human emotions. However, a leader has learned that emotions are temporary, results are long-lasting. Keeping your emotions in check has a great effect on producing the result you want to achieve. A leader understands this and maintains a positive attitude.

In previous chapters I've referred to parents as leaders. This chapter probably rings just as true to parents and spouses. Practice being the emotional thermostat in your house, keeping the positive vibe on an even keel.

# Chapter 16
# Think Creatively

A leader is known for thinking outside-the-box. Look at Richard Branson, Elon Musk or a host of others often featured in the news for their next "crazy idea". Those of us listening may call it crazy; but, they see themselves as visionaries, innovators and creatives. They create concepts that influence the laggers years later. They take their creativity and become innovators who lead early adopters who then get the laggers on board once they see proof that the crazy idea works.
Let's look back at the story I shared earlier about going to Costa Rica to cover a story. Not only was I courageous enough to ask, I was also creative enough to see the result I wanted: travel, and a solution that I could present to get the desired result.

Once while at an early morning chamber meeting I overheard a man talk about his role to market this new restaurant. He said that amidst all the new restaurants opening he was challenged; his prospective diners were hearing too much noise and had too many options. I patiently waited until he was done speaking with the person he was sharing this with. When they were finished with their conversation, I introduced myself (just by name, not by spewing my "sales pitch" on him!). I admitted that I overheard his previous conversation and would like to hear more about his restaurant.

This is where creativity comes in. I was in the midst of writing my book, *The Spontaneous Journey,* and hashtagged it, gaining many Twitter followers who loved food, travel and my adventurous spirit. I was an effective marketer and knew I could help him. Yet, I wasn't a local and didn't have a restaurant background.

Ignoring those facts, I presented an idea to him. I suggested he give me a sizable gift card to spend at the restaurant; while I ate there during the times he was struggling to draw a crowd, I would tweet and see if I could increase traffic. It worked well! Within an hour I had a food blogger and the local TV station sharing the tweet. And, a bonus for the restaurant was that I went back several more times and paid out of my own pocket. In addition, I continued to tweet and promote them because I truly enjoyed the experience, the food, and the attentive staff.

I can share many creative ideas I've had that have resulted in income and other perks. But, the point is that leaders create possibility through being creative. A leader intentionally carves out time to find space to create. He generates ideas, thoughts, and entire new business concepts through his creative thought processes and intentionally creating space for the creativity to flow.

There is an abundance of stories that show how leaders have increased employee engagement, improved communication, and have been rewarded handsomely in terms of financial reward simply through being creative.

It's been said that unless you are the lead dog in the pack, the view is the same. A true leader doesn't have the same view as others; he creates the view that others follow!

# Chapter 17
# Exude Confidence

You've often heard "Fake it til you make it!" or "Act as if......"

To be a leader others must see you as a leader. You must exude the confidence of a leader. If you are unsure of yourself others will find it hard to follow you. So how can you give the outward sign that you are a leader??

Here are some tips that can help boost your confidence:
Dress professionally
Shine those shoes
Wear clothes that are in good repair and free of wrinkles
Darker colored clothes can make you feel powerful
Be clean: for men be clean-shaven and for both men and women have clean nails
Be memorable. Let your personality shine!
Smile
Walk tall
Dress for the occasion
Be well-spoken

These tips boil down to a few areas that can profoundly increase your confidence. Obviously the way you are dressed matters because first impressions count. How you are dressed greets others before you do! Therefore, being well dressed, clean, and appropriate for the occasion immediately captures the attention of the room.

Equally important is your body language as you approach people. This includes your smile which brings warmth and genuineness to every encounter. As momma said, head up and shoulders back. Your posture will display either a lack of confidence or a high level of confidence, whether assumed or genuine. Your posture and smile can truly help you "fake it til you make it". Lastly, if greeting someone in a professional setting or for the first time, offer a firm grip when shaking hands. These body language secrets can provide presumed confidence.

Finally, make every effort to become well-spoken. A larger vocabulary helps you increase your ability to mingle in a room of people at all levels of education. Take your first step by learning one new word each day over the course of a month. As a bonus, this may increase your intelligence. Despite whether you've been a leader for a day or decades, there may come a time where you are in a situation that you aren't comfortable showing leadership ability, yet are required to. Remembering these tips will help you gain composure and assume the role as a confident leader.

# Chapter 18
# Have Integrity

There have been times I've been asked to compromise my integrity and although it was sometimes tempting due to the money you could make or the position you could acquire, it was not worth it. As I've interviewed leaders for my podcast, I've heard them often say they've been asked to compromise. Or, perhaps, they've worked for a company that didn't align with their personal values and way of doing business. This can create a lack of integrity.

During one consulting assignment I was transforming a team, implementing policies and procedures so the business could scale, and had increased revenue by double digits within 60 days when I discovered the owner was hiding revenue and commissions. The intent was that the consulting assignment would go from being a short-term gig to me taking over as CEO. The potential for career advancement and profit sharing was high. But, when I found out the owner was not operating with integrity, I immediately left. This was financially costly to me. However, a leader's reputation can be ruined in an instant.

Oftentimes a lack of integrity is not that severe. Some of my peers have shared stories where their priorities and values simply didn't align well with the company. This caused an imbalance in their work-life balance, friction among co-workers, and other mildly irritating results. Despite the minor irritations, they could have chosen to stay. However, the differences wear on your morale, and sometimes that price isn't worth it.

Sometimes you are surrounded with those that are comfortable delivering less-than-excellent results. Perhaps they turn in projects late or they are often late to work with yet another excuse as to why. One person of influence I interviewed said, *"An excuse is simply a lie you tell yourself when you have fear about a situation."* Using the word "lie" doesn't sugar coat it! When we make excuses we aren't taking responsibility. Lying to ourselves will not allow us to operate with integrity, produce excellent results, and become the leader we are capable of becoming.

Excuses set limits on our performance, our leadership, and our reputation. However, integrity removes those limits allowing us to achieve our full potential.

Integrity is simply doing what you say you will do in the time you said you would do it. Unspoken integrity can be seen as doing what's expected of you whether you are directly asked to own the task or not. Take a look at both of these to see where you can operate with a higher degree of integrity in each area of your life.

# Chapter 19
# Inspire Others

A true leader is never stingy or self-absorbed. They look to impact the lives of others. Most leaders I've interviewed that are recognized by how they've influenced others, inspire by both mentoring and being a mentor, and most importantly sharing with others.

Inspiration comes from conversations with others. These conversations should include transparency, authenticity, encouragement, and wisdom. Professionals that teach you how to craft your story often coach you to share a personal adversity, roadblock, or challenge you faced and how you overcame it. When you do this you inspire others, giving them hope that they too can overcome.

I can't tell you how often I've spoken with successful people, and as they share their story, they tell me that someone else believed in them before they believe in themselves. They were inspired by someone else believing in them and sharing why. Someone took the time to get to know them and find untapped potential in them. Without this boost of inspiration, they often wouldn't have recognized the pivotal moment that propelled them forward with velocity.

Oftentimes a leader inspires others simply by modeling the behaviors of leadership. In conversation with an accomplished executive in higher education, she shared with me two pivotal conversations in her career. First, she watched the Chancellor in action and admired the way she communicated with everyone. The Chancellor exuded ease, confidence, and grace as she spoke both to individuals and during presentations. By watching the Chancellor exhibit qualities she wanted to acquire, she was inspired.

I remember a time when I was staying with a friend, Amy. As I watched Amy interact with others I noticed the ease, confidence, and clarity in which Amy intentionally communicated. It prompted me to inquire how she accomplished that. Today Amy is still a mentor to me, inspiring me to be a better communicator.

The second pivotal moment for this highly successful person in higher education was being told she needed to pursue her Master's Degree because she was capable of it. It hadn't crossed her mind until she was literally told to! Purely because of the respect she had for the person who told her that, she acted with urgency and earned her degree.

We never know when we may say something that inspires someone to achieve greater heights which they are capable of. It may be something said in a presentation, a comment made privately to you, or by modeling the behaviors of a leader; but, one thing is certain, your leadership is inspiring others!

When my radio show took a hiatus, people continued to send messages that a certain episode inspired them. This alone inspired me to relaunch the show. Your impact can be through direct or indirect contact.

# Chapter 20
# Be Approachable

Oftentimes those that see themselves as inferior to leaders don't find leaders approachable. Whereas a peer, another accomplished leader, finds other leaders approachable. Why the disparity in opinion as to whether a leader is approachable or not? I'd sum it up in one word: confidence. Those who are embarrassed by the lack of what they've accomplished do not see themselves as a leader. They haven't achieved the unknown quantity of success they feel they need to call themselves a leader.

Although leaders admittedly say they sometimes lack confidence, they are also confident enough to surround themselves with other leaders. They approach other leaders and other leaders approach them. Leaders know you become who you hang around. One mentor half-jokingly told me, *"I had to trade up my friends."* This is not to say that everyone you meet isn't important. It's simply to say you must protect your time and your mindset and make sure you are hanging out with those that improve you.

Once you build up the confidence to approach other leaders, you will find they are very approachable and willing to invest time in you. Every leader I've met or interviewed has said that success didn't happen alone and they had others who believed in them and invested in them. Because of this they want to give back. They want to mentor others! And if you approach them and ask, oftentimes they will.

I remember when I started my copywriting business. At first I would take smaller jobs with subject matter I was comfortable with. I also undercharged----by a lot. I was starving! I knew two copywriters who were good at their craft. I asked them to sit down with me and teach me about formatting, pricing, how to find clients, and other questions that came up. This information was invaluable to me still being in business today and charging a livable wage.

You may think, *"Why would they help you? You are their competition!"* But, you see, that's where leaders, confident in their ability and operating from a mentality of abundance, are different. They gladly advised me. Occasionally they would even review my work and make suggestions before I sent the finished version to the client.

Today my business is thriving and I owe it to those two successful ladies who were approachable and willing to give back to help someone else succeed.

This is not an anomaly; this is standard practice for those who are truly leaders and recognize their success didn't happen without the help of others.

One friend of mine makes it a point to give away an hour a week of free coaching. Why? Becauses he's successful and wants others to succeed.

# Chapter 21
# Be Committed

Be committed! This is a critical component of leadership.

What does a leader have to be committed to? First, to himself. Without being committed to yourself, chances are you aren't committed to anything. It's like loving others…..to truly love others you must first love yourself.

After being committed to yourself, the list extends to your family, your team, your values, your goals, your time, your mentees, your superiors, and your emotional, spiritual, and physical health. One highly successful mentor of mine said that as you increase capacity in one area, all areas increase. I would say the same for decreasing capacity too. Letting one of these areas fall causes several to fall; causing one area to rise will cause all to rise.

I've seen leaders who are committed in most areas, sometimes letting other areas go. This infiltrates inefficiencies into the areas you are committed to. An example of this that's easy to spot is your physical health. How often have you seen a leader who excels in almost every area of his life, but let's his health go? He's overweight, eating poorly, and not finding time to exercise. This decision will eventually allow him to miss work or not be able to play with his children.

Another area leaders struggle to stay committed to is time. They lose balance between work, family, and friends. Oftentimes, family gets the short end of the stick and they look back and realize this years later.

High-performing leaders usually stay committed to their goals, thus they are high-performing. Occasionally, they may lose temporary sight of a goal because other more urgent demands are placed on them. But, keeping your eye on your goal and staying committed to it is crucial as a leader.

Obviously, I have only touched on a few areas where it's critical to stay committed. But, if you take every area of your life and write down your commitment to that area, you'll quickly be able to do a self-check to see if you are on track for what's important to you.

*"Unless commitment is made, there are only promises and hopes; but no plans."--Peter F. Drucker*

# Chapter 22
# Delegate

Can you become successful alone? All successful people will answer with a resounding "NO!"

Do we all have equal amounts of time in a day? All will say "YES!"

It is not about how much time we have; it's about how we manage our time.
As a successful person climbs to greater heights, they find that they must let go of things they used to have time to do. It's not that they can't do the mundane, daily activities. It's that with a higher degree of success and leadership, they are called to be high-level thinkers ...the visionaries, if you will.

A leader spends his time at the 30,000 foot view getting his team to the next milestone of achievement. But, to accomplish this he must be willing to delegate.

A mentor of mine once gave me this piece of advice, "*You always hire out what you can pay someone to do for less than you make. You always delegate the tasks that aren't essential for you to do.*" This will free up time and keep you in the conversation to lead.

If delegating is necessary, why is it so hard for leaders to actually do? Research has shown there are three primary reasons delegating is hard:

You are still accountable for the results. If you delegate a task and it isn't carried out on time, to completion, or with excellence you are still accountable for it. This can create a problem once it's revealed that who you delegated it to was unable to complete it as expected.

It takes mentoring. A leader delegates to free up his time, yet he finds himself taking time to mentor and train someone to complete the task upholding the same standards he would to complete it himself. This can seem like double the work, rather than offloading some of the work and buying time back.

Loss of control. Leaders don't get to where they are without learning to control their environment, the situation, and many other factors. It can be hard to give up control of how and how well a task is carried out.

Despite these three reasons leaders find it hard to delegate, they will also confide that it is a must!

*"Deciding what not to do is as important as deciding what to do."*--- *Jessica Jackley, co-founder of Kiva*

*"If you really want to grow as an entrepreneur, you've got to learn to delegate."* — *Richard Branson*

# Chapter 23
# Focus

Focus. It's hard for me to preach on focus. As I write this chapter, I admit to having skipped a couple of chapters ahead to tend to this one. And, as an entrepreneur I can also admit to losing focus. Entrepreneurs have a tendency to go from one thing to the next without completion and to touch a project multiple times before making any progress, let alone completing it.

Another challenge for an entrepreneur is the fact that there are so many balls in the air that sometimes he isn't able to juggle everything. The pressure of getting things done on time seems to demand that he work on "a little of this, a little of that". But, that is often counterproductive to what he hopes to have happen.

Finally, an entrepreneur fights the demands of tasks that require him to be out of his element. This can lead to frustration and procrastination which deters from a focused, concentrated effort.

Unfortunately, leaders within organizations fight these same battles. Unreasonable demands, pressure, time-crunched deadlines, and staff discord can draw an executive off-task quickly.

But, what happens when you focus??

Let me share a time when I put unwavering, concentrated effort on a project. On October 8th, I made a commitment to relaunch my podcast that laid dormant for more than six months. I set a goal that I thought was a stretch goal, but achievable, to book twelve guests in three months. That would result in me being able to release one podcast a week to build a consistent listening audience. In the podcast world, one show a week is typical and results in a loyal following. Since I didn't even have a guest on my radar to invite on the show, I thought this would stretch me while helping me focus on consistency.

Here's what happened when I focused. By October 24th I had booked sixteen guests. A week later I had more than thirty guests, including four recording artists on tour! As a music lover, I've had some up-and-coming artists or regionally successful singer-songwriters on my show so I was thrilled when a manager found me and asked me to feature four artists he represents on my show.

In addition to booking more than thirty guests in less than four weeks, I also secured three sponsors and added value to the sponsors by committing to releasing two shows per week instead of the intended one per week. And, if that's not enough, I was invited to be a guest on three other podcasts!

A bit of focused effort catapulted my business to the next level in a matter of weeks! That's what it can do for you. Want better results? Focus!!

# Chapter 24
# Be Bold!

I recall a time when a speaker came in. This speaker impacted both my husband and I. I was concerned about my husband's commitment level in our business, at that time an MLM, and thought meeting this speaker would ignite the fire within us. I called the hotel, requested the speaker's room, and to my amazement was put through. The speaker kindly took my call and accepted my invitation to speak with him over breakfast. The next morning husband, baby, and I traveled to the hotel. My husband was pleasantly shocked! From this meeting opportunity…..where I was bold in my request…...this man mentored us and inspired our family for a number of years. Being bold enough to make that call paid dividends in us having a business coach with the acumen we needed, inspiration and hope as we flailed around trying to figure out the business world, and in our income.

Everyone of us has a desire to be bold! Some of us go for it while others shy away from it. If you calculate the risks, believe in yourself, and are committed to your dream, you'll discover your dream is worth the risk! Sometimes the risk won't pay off, other times it will. However, you'll have fewer regrets by being bold and being willing to stick your neck out and try.

Let me share another time I took a risk to heal a relationship. We had business partners and as my marriage was failing, my husband withdrew more and more from the business. This left the partners with more than 50% of the work. Finally, the business ended when the partner's husband and I delivered the last batch of paperwork for our accountant to dissolve the business. The uneasy tension and disappointment could be felt and the meeting happened mainly in silence.

Years later I had the opportunity to reach out through Facebook and request a meeting. He accepted. While meeting he put his wife, also my former partner, on the phone. The three of us were able to mend our relationship and finish this meeting with a hug, laughter, and the promise to meet again.

Being bold can pay dividends in many ways. And in my opinion, relationships are just as valuable as money and business opportunities.

Richard Branson took a risk when he financed Virgin Airlines with the profits from Virgin Music. Elon Musk has taken risk and scorn looking at alternative ways to power our cars. The Hyperloop concept is a risk in transforming the way we travel.

Some ideas fail. Others succeed. But, none succeed without someone being bold enough to take a risk!

*"There are risks and costs to action. But they are far less than the long range risks of comfortable inaction."--- John F. Kennedy*

# Chapter 25
# Have Passion

Passion! Have you ever tried to follow someone without passion? Imagine the old "dry eyes" commercial as you sit in your meeting with the president of your company. Imagine your marriage without any passion.
Passion exists to enroll others in your ideas, your business, and your life!

Without passion you are lacking the zest of life. Without passion you lack the fire to lead.

*"There's so much about Dolly Parton that every female artist should look to, whether it's reading her quotes or reading her interviews or going to one of her live shows. She's been such an amazing example to every female songwriter out there."--- Taylor Swift*

Whether you like or dislike Dolly Parton and country music, there is no denying Dolly does everything with gusto. Her bold voice spellbounds the room and people know she is there. She has built a music empire and a business empire. Her success has inspired others, like Taylor Swift, to use their business acumen and create something with passion.

*"Every great dream begins with a dreamer. Always remember, you have within you the strength, patience, and the passion to reach for the stars to change the world."---Harriet Tubman*

*"There is no passion to be found playing small--in settling for a life that is less than the one you are capable of living."---Nelson Mandela*

*"Develop a passion for learning. If you do, you will never cease to grow."---Anthony J. D'Angelo*

*"Passion is energy. Feel the power that comes from focusing on what excites you."----Oprah Winfrey*

Your family, friends, co-workers, and peers are watching. Will you show them how to live with passion?

I remember a time when I received feedback that my speeches were somewhat monotone, yet they could see the passion in me. After some testing of the brain waves they found that it is a medical condition without a solution. However, people still see my passion and my commitment to living life fully. Every day I wake up to opportunities in my life and almost daily I get a message that I am encouraging someone through my sharing. Don't make excuses and let what's so stop you from being what can be.

You will only go down in the history books of life if you live passionately. As Nelson Mandela asks, "Are you settling for a life that is less than you are capable of living?"

# Chapter 26
# Resilience

Resilience and persistence are sometimes used interchangeably; but, there is a difference. Let's begin by defining that difference.

Resilience: the capacity to recover quickly from difficulties; toughness

Persistence: firm or obstinate continuance in a course of action in spite of difficulty or opposition
They both deal with difficulty and require a mindset to be mentally tough; however, resilience refers to bouncing back and persistence refers to pressing on.

During my years as an entrepreneur, I learned to press on when people told me I should get a job. I learned to press on when I was told "no" over and over again. That's persistence (more on that in the next chapter). But, resilience was my ability to recover when I lost everything. During the recession of 2008 I was in the real estate business, and unaware of the warning signs soon enough to get out or protect my assets. The result: I filed bankruptcy. That could have devastated me enough that I refused to start another business. Instead I spent a couple of years in a job stabilizing my income long enough to recover.

The second total loss was during my divorce; I was left with no home, no alimony, no insurance, and I lost my contract the same week, which meant no income. I had nothing! Resilience meant getting out of bed every morning and rebuilding. I had to excuse the thoughts of a victim mentality and adopt the thinking of a victor. I had succeeded before; I could succeed again. That's resilience!

*"Resilience is, of course, necessary for a warrior......"--- Phil Klay*

*"Resilience is all about being able to overcome the unexpected. Sustainability is about survival. The goal of resilience is to thrive."-- - Jamais Cascio*

My radio show, *Thrive: A Woman's Journey to Victory*, was named because I believe our goal isn't only to survive but THRIVE. That's what you are destined to do!!

You will have unexpected challenges that you will have to overcome; but, I promise you without the resilience to overcome, you will look back on your life with disappointment and defeat. With resilience you will look back and see how small the challenges really were and how courageous you were for moving past them.

# Chapter 27
# Persistence

Persist with the system. That's right! If you keep doing it over and over again with a system that gets results, you will win! Mark Cuban tells us in his book, *How To Win At The Sport Of Business*, that we must persist and get our core competencies and execution right before expanding. Without focus and persistence on what we are already doing, we will spread ourselves too thin and accomplish nothing.

As a coach tells an athlete, practice the basics, get good at the basics, PERSIST with the basics. There are fundamentals in sports and business. Only by persisting until you get the fundamentals right, can you WIN!

*"Nothing in this world can take the place of persistence. Talent will not: nothing is more common than unsuccessful men with talent. Genius will not; unrewarded genius is almost a proverb. Education will not: the world is full of educated derelicts. Persistence and determination alone are omnipotent."--Calvin Coolidge*

Mark Cuban also validates this, sharing times when more than one person "had the manual"; but, because he read the manual he succeeded. They all had access to equal talent and genius with the same manual; however, because he persisted and followed directions, making MicroSolutions successful.

You've often heard the phrase *"One more time! Just give it one more try!"* Well, it's true.

*"Success is not the absence of failure; it's the persistence through failure."-- Aisha Tyler*

There's a list of entrepreneurs who tried and failed, again and again, before succeeding: Colonel Sanders, Henry Ford, and Bill Gates are recent examples. We could go back to Thomas Edison who failed more than 3,000 times before giving us the light bulb or the Wright Brothers who persisted for three years. Now thanks to them we have thousands of flights per day!

I too have had to persist. I've owned nearly a dozen businesses and some have failed while others have succeeded. I don't believe I've been my most successful yet and it's the persistence that will get me there. I persist in daily habits, a winning mindset, the systems I've put in place for my business, networking, learning something new everyday, and other keys to drive me down the path of success for my business.

Being an entrepreneur takes fortitude. It's not for the faint of heart or the risk averse. It takes one who persists against the odds, against the feelings and emotions that can take you on a roller coaster ride if you allow it, and against those nay-sayers who tell you it won't or can't happen.

Persist! Persist! Persist! And when you feel like giving up, persist one more time!

# Bonus Chapters

Stories originally published on SelfGrowth.com

A Look Back At 2015

As I look back on 2015, I think "Wow! What an amazing year!" Yes, it had some challenges and disappointments. No, my income wasn't as high as I had planned. But, I can look back and say it was truly an amazing year and I am blessed beyond belief. Let me recap to explain why.

In January I began on a cruise with a group of about 60 people who were looking to take life up a notch. And, boy, did we! Many of us on that cruise have co-written a book on thriving that is about to be released.

In February I traveled to Nashville for the first time. This city is a city I have longed to go to for many years. It is a vibrant city for many reasons other than the obvious reason of being called "Music City". The foodie culture is evident in every neighborhood. The entrepreneurial spirit is alive and well. While there I attended several startup events, attended business seminars, and toured coworking spaces. From that came two **business opportunities**.

First, I was asked to travel to Costa Rica to cover a story for Soles4Souls, which Kim Kardashian recently gave a large donation to. I covered that story in May. After meeting the marketing manager for a new restaurant, I was asked to Tweet during a slow night. Within an hour NashTV and a national food blogger followed the tweets. Success!

February also marks the month I released my first book, *7 Beautiful Weeks: The Love Affair That Wasn't Meant to Last*. Not a bad year, and we are only two months in.

In April I return to Orlando to judge for the DECA International Collegiate Business Plan Competition. This was not only a highlight because my **passion** is mentoring college students; but, in **networking** with the other judges I met one in particular that would become instrumental later in the year.

In June I relocated for the summer and lived "the beach life". This happened because in February I visited an out-of-state friend when I saw a Facebook post of another friend about a Startup Weekend an hour away from the friend I was visiting. I quickly drove down to help mentor for the Startup Weekend. Through **networking** an offer was presented for me to help startups get "off the ground" and lead a group of interns. I was living the dream: coaching **entrepreneurs**, mentoring bright, young students, and living on the beach.

With the beach life over, the story of the other judge for the DECA competition comes back into sight. When we met part of our conversation revolved around him sharing his trip to Italy to meet family and my desire to go to Italy. It was now time to book that long-awaited trip, and I reached out to let him know. He connected me with one of his family members there. We connected and because of this connection, I not only had advice, but a host, tour guide, and eventually a friend. **Networking** enriches your life and you never know where it will lead.

While in Italy, I published book number two, *The Spontaneous Journey*, which was written about the 10-week long adventures I had earlier in the Spring, covering one of my favorite cities, Nashville.

I spent a month in Italy and returned just in time to celebrate Christmas. Christmas has always been my favorite holiday. And this Christmas I got to celebrate twice since both of my children live in different cities.

In conclusion, I could choose to focus on the few disappointments or I can recall the wonderful memories from visiting 3 different countries and several new states. I can count the numerous friends I have made along the way. I can look at the thousands of pictures I took while journaling my travels and know that I am blessed.

Leadership Knows No Age

Leadership comes in all ages and knows no boundaries. I had the privilege of being invited to join Ohio State University athletes (Go Buckeyes! was the cheer) and Soles4Souls on a shoe distribution to Costa Rica.

The athletes may be from the same campus; however, most of them didn't know one another. The ride from the airport to the "home base" in Costa Rica was relatively quiet and uneventful.

The first day of distribution these athletes began to show the promise of leadership as they stepped up to the plate and interacted with the children, stooped down for several hours to fit shoes, and lift numerous boxes of shoes in the heat.

The second day's distribution was even more cohesive for the team. Each had identified their **leadership skills** well. Some used their athletic ability and took the initiative to play jump rope or soccer with a group of children longing to interact with these "kind strangers from a different country". Others shined with their organizational skills creating order as we greeted, sized, and fit over 800 children in just over 4 hours.

By this second evening the group had clearly gone from strangers on the same campus to friends. They shared bags of chips, took turns DJing and sharing their musical interests, and showing genuine interest in each other. Leaders take a genuine interest and do more listening than talking. These simple acts show the promise of a true leader.

As we readied the team for a long trek up to the rain forest, fear came out in some of the students. Some afraid of water, others afraid of meeting an unwanted animal. Each student took the opportunity to comfort and encourage the others to overcome their fear. After all, athletes train hard and push through many challenges to overcome obstacles. Fears are just another obstacle that can be overcome by the power of the mind (and some encouragement from a friend). As an onlooker it was truly inspiring to watch each encourage the other. Finally, I was not just an onlooker; but, a recipient of encouragement. I am not fond of ladders. As I approached the first zip of the zip line, There was a vertical ladder spanning about 40 feet high (or I imagined it to be 40 feet high anyway!). Half way up I lost the courage to continue. I quickly had 3 people standing beside me to encourage me. I did overcome and enthusiastically completed the zip line course! That wouldn't have happened had someone not stepped up as a leader and provided the necessary encouragement.

The thing about a leader is sometimes you are leading and other times it's wise to step back and follow the leader. A leader knows when he is capable of leading; but, he also knows when it's best to pass the baton to another leader.

The other ironic thing about leadership is that we continue to develop those skills throughout our life (provided we want to). One of my favorite phrases is "**learning** should be a lifelong process". Leaders learn. Learners become leaders.

Although these Buckeyes were only in their early twenties, and I only spent six short, enjoyable days with them, I look forward to watching them develop into future leaders.

**Opportunity Knocks: Can You Hear It?**

Have you ever heard opportunity knock? Are you aware it knocks in large and small ways every day?

I was banging on the door of an organization for about 6 months. Nothing happened. I couldn't even get an email returned.
Although I was frustrated, I kept knocking (literally emailing and calling). Oh, and let's not forget social media; I reached out through LinkedIn to several connections. But, to no avail.

As I began what I dubbed #theSpontaneousJourney I sat in Alabama. Visiting a friend, working on my writing assignments, and just relaxing. After all, there isn't much to do as far as **networking** opportunities in this part of Alabama. Suddenly, I saw a post on social media for an opportunity to attend an event with this organization in Nashville. That just happened to be my next stop on #theSpontaneousJourney and I would be there at the time of this event! How fortuitous.

As I eagerly awaited the day in Nashville I made sure I cleared my calendar for the day after to follow up with any good leads. During the evening of the event, I made a few good connections.

One connection led to a meeting, a story, and then a bigger opportunity. I will be going to Costa Rica to cover a very cool story with another organization next month!

I used Airbnb to travel and heard opportunity knock in small ways, too. I spent a few nights with five college students from Brazil and the UK. Two of them missed their dogs and the companionship a dog provides. Because I was traveling with my dog they had the chance to play with mine. The smile that put on their faces was priceless.

I spent the night in the home of someone that housed a foster child. She and I had several hours to talk. I was able to answer "opportunity" by feeding hope into this young life through the conversations we had. She thanked me by bringing me a homemade treat from a celebration she had with friends. That small gesture showed me I impacted her life in a small way just by being available.

Although I am back home, I wouldn't say #theSpontaneousJourney has ended yet. Opportunity knocked several times while on the road. The results of me recognizing when opportunity was knocking are still playing out.

Whether opportunity knocks in a big way, such as going to another country to cover a story, or in a small way such as spending a few nights in the same house with a foster child and feeding hope into their lives through conversation, opportunity knocks daily. Are you listening for it? Will you answer the door? Are you willing to take the "risk"?

Because I used Airbnb to travel, I met people from all over the world with diverse backgrounds. I stayed with **yoga** instructors, world travelers, songwriters, foster children, project managers, salespeople, and so many others. Where can you connect with so many types of people. I have stories to tell for years to come. And, I had opportunities I would never have had sitting on my couch at home.

It's worth it to take risks. Take a leap of **faith** and open the door to opportunity. I encourage you to recognize opportunity, answer its knock, and take your own journey. It won't look anything like mine because it's yours. Go on, answer the door. Opportunity is knocking.

### Leadership: Valentine's Day Style

(Why did I include this in a leadership book? Statistics tell us there are 1 in 4 women who have been abused. My goal is to help you realize you don't have to continue to live in that reality.)

Sometimes lessons in leadership come from the most unlikely places; when you look for life's lessons, it's amazing where you will find them. I have found them in the small details, the fleeting moments, and the major life-changing transitions. As Valentine's Day approaches, I want to share some leadership lessons from a love story.

Sometimes your most intimate relationships are a mirror for the other relationships in your life. As our grandmother always told us, you become like the five people you spend most of your time with. If they are angry, you tend to be angry. If they have a positive outlook on life, you probably do, too.

There was a couple who had dated a short time. After the initial "honeymoon" phase of **dating** was over, the relationship began to take a drastic turn in the conversations. Over several weeks a pattern emerged. The man was affectionate and inviting the girlfriend to meet him. Once together, the conversation turned toward criticism, anger, and their differences which he viewed with contempt. Afterwards, the texts would read like nothing was awry.

A thought resonates with me from a book I've read and re-read the past few months: your truth is NOT determined by someone else's opinion. **Abuse** is typically viewed in terms of domestic violence or physical **abuse**. However, someone that attempts to make you feel inferior is toxic (and if you let it continue, can be emotionally abusive) to you. Whether in business or personal relationships, these people should be removed from or limited in contact.

Maybe you feel this can't or doesn't happen in a business environment. Nevertheless, let me share a personal story from my career. When I worked in a commissioned environment a co-worker approached me and proceeded to berate me for approaching "her" customer. Confronting someone in business is okay, and even necessary; however, it must be done in a respectful manner. I asked my colleagues to come off the selling floor with me, and told her that anytime we had a conflict to settle it must be done in private and with respect for each other. That was the last time we had a problem. Some people just need to know that you know your worth, and that you will not allow them to diminish it.

WE determine our worth by what we are willing to accept. What do you accept at work? In your home? In your relationships? Equally important, how do you make people feel when they are around you?

You determine what you are worth by what you are willing to accept. Walk off the "clearance rack" and put yourself on the shelf where "valuables" are kept. And value others.

As we celebrate Valentine's Day, love yourself enough to evaluate your relationships, remove the toxic ones, and put yourself on the "valuables" shelf. When your truth says you are worthy, you will begin to move in the direction of your goals.

## Hibernating

Hibernating (from the cold).....What's it good for??

As I travel on my spontaneous journey, I am eager to see the places I am visiting. I have made some sacrifices to take this journey so I want to get all the pleasure from it I can. I am currently in the city I was most looking forward to visiting, Nashville. Not only do I like warm weather, I also like live music (and yes, I'll admit it, country music).

Yet, it's currently in the teens (and for a Florida girl, that's COLD!) after a day of sleet and rain followed by a day of snow. And for my Northern friends, you know what that means...ice. The roads are icy. Many places are closed. Even if they are open, who wants to go out?

Not this warm weather girl!

So as I spend two days in hibernation, I can choose to look at the above situation and be angry and unhappy or I can choose to look at two days of being "home bound" as a blessing. I choose to look at it as a blessing.

Being in hibernation gives me time to reflect, set goals and make sure I stay on track for the ones I've already set, check some assignments off my to-do list, and most importantly, be grateful. Not having anywhere to go or a schedule to keep also gives me time to call friends and **family** without the pressure of being interrupted.

Practicing the art of gratitude is important. In the solitude and quiet that I am given while hibernating from the cold, I can take the time to thank my Creator for all the abundant blessings I have been given. There are blessings that are clear like our health or a special person in our lives. But, sometimes we have to look at the small blessings of the precious moments and be grateful. Moments where you watch the sunset or enjoy the smell of freshly brewed coffee or a smile as you recall a text from your friend. When you are grateful for what you already have, I believe it opens up doors to receive more. To validate this I found a book in the home where I am staying called "The Art of Gratitude"; how apropos. I am an avid reader and this book continued to remind me to see **abundance** and practice **gratitude** daily...for the obvious blessings and the small, momentary blessings.

In every circumstance I believe we have a choice. A choice to look at the negative and whine about it or a choice to look at the positive and give thanks. What will you do? For the second consecutive day of hibernation I will choose to give thanks!

## Lessons Learned From A Naked Neighbor

On a Saturday night at home while relaxing with friends, things turned interesting quickly. A dog showed up at the house. In an attempt to find the rightful owner and return the dog, we knocked on the door of the rightful owner and a naked man opened the door. This was the start of an interesting week.

After the man got dressed he came down, supposedly to claim his dog. However, he sat down, made himself at home, and "gifted" us the dog. This is where **attitude**, perspective, integrity, and **wisdom** come in. It takes all of these to walk through the journey that began in this moment. After a brief visit, he left, and we were now the proud owners of this dog. It takes **wisdom** to know that our lifestyle is mismatched for the needs of this dog; the owner that "gifted" us the dog was mismatched for him as well.

Three attempts to return the dog to his naked owner failed. (I think he was avoiding us.) But, because our lifestyle wasn't conducive to giving this poor dog the attention he needed, he wreaked havoc on the neighbors. They got involved. After we shared the story, they gained a new perspective and wisely stepped in to help us find a solution.

One week later it was decided (by neighborhood consensus, I believe) that the dog would be picked up from us by the naked neighbor. He would then return it to the prior owner who was more equipped to care for it. An hour after the dog was picked up, he escaped and returned to us.

When faced with unexpected challenges in life, it helps to see everyone's perspective. The dog's perspective was he obviously was unhappy with his current home and was extremely happy at ours. Our perspective, however, is that we didn't have time to devote to him and give him a proper home. The "naked neighbor's" perspective was that although he was a lonely guy, he didn't have the desire to devote his time to a dog. The obvious lack of affection between he and the dog showed he didn't desire a 4-legged companion to fill his void.

We have to look at one another's perspective to solve a problem with wisdom and integrity. That's the sign of a leader. Although a naked neighbor typically has little to do with leadership, it did bring a neighborhood together to understand one another and work as a team to solve a problem. And, give everyone moments of laughter and a good **attitude**. So, as with everything in life, we can learn from each experience we are given.

**Pondering Life**

As I sit in Europe alone on Thanksgiving, I ponder life's lessons and memories with **family**. Thanksgiving gives us reason to pause and be thankful for what we have and reflect on the fond memories of the past and look with hope to the future.

Thanksgiving is a time of family, friends, happiness, **abundance**, and **gratitude**. Thanksgiving should be a regular habit, not an annual occurrence.

So as I sit admiring the **beauty** of an ancient world and a culture that stands still through time, I share some thoughts with you in this simple poem.

Pondering Life
Pondering life can take you many directions.
Success. Failure. Deep emotions. Happy memories.
Looking to the future life looks bright,
Looking in my past I am blessed,
Looking at the present I enjoy each day.
Life. Sometimes it can be complicated,
Sometimes simple, sometimes simply complicated.
Pondering life can make us feel
Regret, **loneliness**, love, or joy.
But one thing about pondering life
Is your thoughts can take you far away.
As you ponder life paint your **dreams**.
Believe them. Make them true.

I hope you enjoyed the simplicity of "Pondering Life". I have a friend that says "make it true". I want to encourage you to "make it true", whatever you are painting your life to be, pursue it with **passion** and purpose.
Practice the art of Thanksgiving daily.

# That's a Wrap

My hope is that you'll take these secrets (which really aren't' secrets, by the way!) and use them to launch you to the level of leadership you want to accomplish. I urge you to lead to your maximum potential.

Whatever dream, invention, or idea you have that is worthy of pursuing has value. As Nelson Mandela said you can play small and live a life less than you are capable of living or you can be bold, courageous, tenacious, and defy the odds and LEAD!

We are all called to lead to our maximum potential. For some of us that means in our class or among our MBA classmates. For others in our home. And, for others to create the next Google, Apple, or Virgin Airlines. Whatever it is and whoever you are leading, lead them!!

It will take all you've got some days to step up to the plate and bat again. Sometimes you'll get to first base, other times you'll strike out, and sometimes you'll hit a homerun. What you hit isn't as important as the fact that you got up one more time.

Michael Jordan missed three times as many shots as he made, yet he's considered one of the greatest athletes of all time. Babe Ruth struck out three times more than he hit a homerun, yet he too is considered a pioneer in the sports world.

There are times…....let's be honest, years….....I played small. I lived a life less than I was capable of. I mastered the looks and attitudes of pity, poor me, victim, surviving, life is tough, and all the others that go with playing small.

When I began leading to my maximum potential, using the secrets of leadership, and surrounding myself with those who wouldn't accept my excuses to be small, my world changed! I get calls from Europe asking me to speak at conferences. I get introduced to people who want me to take over their business in retirement. I wake up to messages on LinkedIn and email because people have recommended me and those messages result in new clients. And, my kids surprise me and say, *"Mom, you are my hero! You inspire me! You are an example to me in life and business."*

To me that's the greatest gift of all. Whatever your desire to become a better, more effective leader, it is available to you within these secrets.

# Special Acknowledgements

Throughout my life, many have shared ideas, mentored and supported me. I wouldn't be where I am today without them. Although I may forget some, I'd like to thank Susan Greene, Amy Goodman, Marlene Spiegel, Bob Kittridge, Jen Furda, and Sandi Vidal who have impacted my career with their advice, support, and friendship. They have each taught me valuable lessons in business, and today I can say I also value their friendship. There have been hundreds who have impacted my life for a season; knowing I'd forget many, I choose to leave them unnamed.

I have also been impacted by organizations that have taught me leadership and entrepreneurship that I've used in my business through the years. These organizations impacted me as a youth while participating in them and as an adult while volunteering with them. They are 4-H, DECA (Distributive Education Clubs of America), and Junior Achievement.

Most importantly are those closest to me. I have friends who have stood beside me through loss and triumph, adversity and victory, and have never waved in their support. This list (and I hope I don't forget anyone!) includes Karen Johnson, Susan Karol, Connie Justice, Scott Saunders, Kristi Grabill, Kyle Davis, Francis Lampasi, and I must mention Sandi Vidal and Amy Goodman once more.

I'd be remiss if I didn't mention my mom, brother, aunt, and grandma who influenced all my days with their unconditional love and support. And, the loves of my life, my children! I'd like to thank James and Tiffany for being my biggest cheerleaders and understanding the many hours I put into making my business grow. They love me, support me, offer their opinions, and give me the space to put in long hours. Thank you for all you mean to me!!

# About Royce Gomez

Royce Gomez, founder of RoyceTalks, has been recognized as a leading authority for coaching and training entrepreneurs, which has included Ashoka sponsored events at Rollins College, Clinton Global Initiative University changemakers, Startup Weekend participants, business incubators and accelerators, venture pitch competitions, and SBDC events. Her articles have been published in the HuffingtonPost, Carol Roth, and other print and online media platforms. She has effectively coached successful business owners and written content for hundreds of companies. Royce's strategies increase revenue and her content gets results.

Royce started out modeling and in the fashion world before retail management then owning her own business. Since starting her first business, Royce has owned 12 different businesses. As a business coach, she has succeeded in a local storefront business, real estate investing, equine programs, image consulting, and home based businesses. She is a coach who works with business owners, not coaches. Because of extensive background in marketing, Royce has had the opportunity to write copy for Calvin Klein, DoubleTree, Keller Williams, Acti-Labs, Gone to Green and hundreds more.

Royce is the mother of 2 amazing adult children. She is an avid traveler and loves adventure, wine tasting, and music. Recently, she added kayaking as one of her favorite activities.

www.RoyceTalks.com    www.CoachingWithRoyce.com

Royce Gomez